Milky

And

Vine

By

David Brooks &

Vincent Vine

This book is dedicated to all the happy people around the world: You've got no reason not to.

Some peeps are like Slinky's.

Pretty much useless but make u smile,

when u push them down D stairs. :)

David Brooks & Vincent Vine

1f u c4n r34d 7h15,

u r34lly n33d 2 g37 l41d

Milky And Vine

I was at sea D other day & loads of meat floated past.

It was a bit choppy.

David Brooks & Vincent Vine

Smile...

It confuses people..!!

Milky And Vine

Black holes.

I don't know what people see in them.

Exit signs? They're on their way out.

                        David Brooks & Vincent Vine

Practice makes prfect

but thn, nobody is prfect so what's D point of practicing?

Milky And Vine

I saw this train driver & said, 'Hey I wanna go to Paris.' He asked, 'Eurostar?' I said, 'Well I've been on telly but I'm no Dean Martin.' Mind u, at least D Eurostar's comfy. It's murder on D Orient Express isn't it?

David Brooks & Vincent Vine

DN'T HIT KIDS!!!

No, seriously, they have guns now.

David Brooks & Vincent Vine

Life is lik a hot bath.

It feels good while u're in it, but D longer u stay in, D more wrinkled u get.

Milky And Vine

D other day some1 left a piece of plasticine in my dressing room. I didn't know what to make of it.

David Brooks & Vincent Vine

Don't knock on death's door.

Hit D doorbell & run.

He hates that.

Milky And Vine

Why the hell are they called apartments if they're all stuck together?

Milky And Vine

So, I fancied a game of darts with my mate. He said, 'Nearest D bull goes first.' He wnt 'Baah' & I went 'Moo'. He said 'U're closest.'

David Brooks & Vincent Vine

I ran into my x today...

put it in reverse & did it again!!!

Milky And Vine

I wish my book of life ws written in pencil...

There are a few pages I would lik to erase.

David Brooks & Vincent Vine

So, I was getting into my car, & this bloke says to me 'Can u give me a lift?' I said 'Sure, u look great, D world's ur oyster, go for it.'

Milky And Vine

Do not drink & drive

or

u might spill D drink.

David Brooks & Vincent Vine

I saw this bloke chatting up a cheetah.

He was trying to pull a fast one.

Milky And Vine

Whn life gives u lemons,

make grape juice,

then sit back,

& let D world wonder hw u did it.

David Brooks & Vincent Vine

I've got a sponge frnt door.

Hey, dn't knock it.

Milky And Vine

When nothing goes right,

Go left.

David Brooks & Vincent Vine

when life gives u lemons..

Squirt it in ur enemies eyes!!

Milky And Vine

I'm against hunting.

I'm actually a hunt saboteur.

I go out D night before & shoot D fox.

David Brooks & Vincent Vine

I couldn't repair ur brakes,

so, I made ur horn louder.

Milky And Vine

A "Lion" would never cheat on his wife

but a "Tiger Wood".

David Brooks & Vincent Vine

Adults are just kids with money.

Milky And Vine

Relationship Status:

( ) Single

( ) In a relationship

( ) Married

( ) Engaged

( ) Divorced

(x) Waiting for a miracle

David Brooks & Vincent Vine

I am free of all prejudices. I hate everyone equally.

Milky And Vine

I don't have an attitude problem,

u have a perception problem.

David Brooks & Vincent Vine

I went on a diet, stopped smoking dope, cut out D drinking & heavy eating, & in fourteen days

I lost 2 weeks.

Milky And Vine

Don't cry because its over,

smile because his new girlfriend looks like a

horse""

David Brooks & Vincent Vine

I'm fat.

But u're ugly.

At least I can diet.

Milky And Vine

A picture is worth a thousand words, but only if u know that many.

David Brooks & Vincent Vine

So, she smashed her rearview mirror,

cause from now on she's never looking back

Milky And Vine

"U know, somebody actually complimented me on my driving today.

They left a little note on D windscreen, it said 'Parking Fine.'

So that was nice."

David Brooks & Vincent Vine

Don't kiss by D garden gate,

love is blind,

but D neighbors ain't.

Milky And Vine

Of all D things I've lost,

I miss my mind D most.

David Brooks & Vincent Vine

When God made me,

he was showing off!!

Milky And Vine

I phoned D local gym & I asked if they could teach me how to do D splits.

He said, "How flexible are u?"

I said, "I can't make Tuesdays."

David Brooks & Vincent Vine

Life is a game with a small fault…

there is no "restart button" in it.

Milky And Vine

People want what they can't have & when they get it they don't want it anymore.

David Brooks & Vincent Vine

I met this gangster who pulls up people's pants.

Name's Wedgie Kray.

Milky And Vine

People have told me to never say never – they broke their own rule!

David Brooks & Vincent Vine

Why is there no egg in eggplant & no ham in hamburger?

Milky And Vine

Believe it or not, there are twice as many eyebrows in D world as there are people.

David Brooks & Vincent Vine

I turned my phone onto "Airplane mode" & threw it up into D air.

Worst Transformer Ever.

Milky And Vine

So many men & yet so few brains.

David Brooks & Vincent Vine

"THE IMPOSSIBLE..." what nobdy can do until somebody does.......

Milky And Vine

D universe contains protons, neutrons, electrons & morons. U one? Hell NO!

David Brooks & Vincent Vine

If karma doesn't come around & hit u in D face,

I will.

Milky And Vine

A brain has two parts: D left part & D right part.

My left brain has nothing right, while my right brain has nothing left.

David Brooks & Vincent Vine

Why do people say life is short?

Live D longest thing u could ever do...

Milky And Vine

Made in the USA
Lexington, KY
23 December 2017